Brinsford books

Knife edge

by Ann Ruffell

AXIS education

30109 05122423 9

Acknowledgements

Illustrations: Tim Neale

The 2005 editions of Brinsford books were published as a direct result of the findings of a two-year authoring project at HMYOI Brinsford near Wolverhampton. Brinsford books have been so hugely popular that this second series is a derivative of the 2005 books. Grateful thanks go to all the young people who participated so enthusiastically in the original project and to Judy Jackson and Brian Eccleshall of Dudley College.

First published in Great Britain by Axis Education Ltd

ISBN 978-1-84618-086-6

Axis Education PO Box 459

Shrewsbury SY4 4WZ

Email:enquiries@axiseducation.co.uk

www.axiseducation.co.uk

Printed by The Cromwell Press, Trowbridge, Wiltshire.

Chapter 1

Troy head-butted the boy in the playground.

John had been annoying him for months. He was the sort of kid that got everything right. He always had his hand up before everyone else. He always got the answer right. Troy hated him. If Troy put his hand up the teacher would sigh and say, "What now, Troy?" The teachers never even asked if he knew the answers. He never did, but that wasn't the point.

He knew what would happen now. A teacher would come out of the staffroom and he'd get punished.

Troy didn't care. Let them all come out. Let them punish him. They'd only put him outside the classroom door. Then he could mess up all the stuff pinned up on the corridor walls.

At least people noticed him. All the kids were scared of him. He liked that. He liked being big.

At home if he got on the wrong side of his stepdad he would get hammered. They weren't allowed to hammer him at school. His brother told him that kids have got rights. If they even touch you, you can take them to court.

There wasn't a law about brothers hammering you. Or if there was, his brother hadn't told Troy about it.

Troy would have asked his mum if he could. But he hardly ever saw his Mum. When he got home Mum was already in the pub, and she never got up before he had to go to school. Maybe that was a good thing. Mum could hit harder than both his brother and his stepdad. Troy had given up trying to do what she wanted, because he always seemed to be wrong.

He left school to go on the dole. They tried to make him go to college to get some exams. "They give you £30 just to be there."

What was the point? It was easier to doss around. His new stepdad was a wimp. His brother had left home. Now that he was nearly 6 foot tall his Mum didn't hit him any more. She had tried once, but never again.

And out on the streets he was a big man. He'd been banned from a lot of the pubs and clubs, but so what? They were poncy places. He liked the ones where you could have a good fight and they'd let you back in again.

He was good with a knife, too. Quick, accurate. £30 to go to college? That was a joke. It was easier to take a few quid from someone who was loaded. Troy was pretty good with the machete too. There were drug dealers out there who would fleece you for a gram of smack. They soon learned that trying to take Troy for a ride was not a good idea.

No one messed with Troy Callan.

Then his best mate Zack asked him to go to this football club with him.

Chapter 2

"Don't be stupid," said Troy. "I don't do clubs. Only night clubs." And he laughed to show Zack what he meant.

"No, come on. It will be cool. You don't have to stay if you don't want to. It's free."

"Do you get free dope?" said Troy with a grin.

Zack laughed too. "I wish!" he said.

It seemed a bit pointless at first, just running up and down a field. A bit like stuff for kids, but he was fit and it wasn't raining. They had numbers – okay, just like a proper team – and there was the same number of balls. You had to pass the ball to the next number up. Like, he was number 3, and he had to kick the ball to number 4. Easy. He couldn't see why other people thought it was hard. Some of them were kicking the balls all over the place.

"Troy, number 4, not 11!"

Oh, yeah, very funny. He had mistimed the kick. Next time he slammed the ball over the field. But no one seemed to notice his temper. Number 4 ran for it, and Troy booted the ball from number 2 coming at him.

"Nice one, number 3!" The coach was running past. Gave him the thumbs up.

It had been a fluke. He'd only just seen it out of the corner of his eye. But he'd got it, and passed it over to number 4 who was back on the field.

He felt a glow. Never felt like that before. When the coach told them to use only their left feet this time, he did it. Perfect. The coach was over the other side of the field, so no thumbs up this time. He didn't need it. He knew he'd done it right.

The two hours were over before he knew it. Funny. Time usually dragged unless he was in a pub sinking several pints.

The best bit of it had been when Bob Gregg, the club manager, walked onto the pitch, just before they'd finished.

He nodded at Troy. "Nice footwork." That was all. But how long had it been since someone had said he'd done anything 'nice'?

Only all his life.

When they were changing back into their jeans he realised he'd had the best morning of his life.

"Hey, you were good, man," said Zack. He chucked his muddy boots into a plastic Tesco bag.

"Yeah? You too, man." Troy felt dead chuffed.

"Coming next week?"

"If I haven't got a hangover. We're going to Shades, Friday night, remember?"

Shades was a great night club. Plenty of draw and smack. The bouncers were scared of them so they never got slung out. He'd be ratted before midnight. There would probably be a fight – there always was. He'd take a couple of knives with him, to protect himself.

Whatever happened, he'd need a whole day to sleep it off.

"Tell you what, Zack. Why don't we go Saturday night instead?"

The next Saturday football session was not so good. Troy couldn't understand why he had to think of anyone else.

"Pass it to Mark, Troy!"

Troy was bombing down the pitch. They should be praising him, not telling him off. He was faster than anyone else. He'd got the ball under control. What else did they want?

"You want the ball to go into the goal, right?" he argued. "That's what I'm doing!"

How come nobody could see it his way?

They had a pep talk from the coach after the training. The coach gathered them round, panting and mud-spattered, before they went back to the changing room.

"This is the first thing you've got to learn," he said. "You can have all the star players you like, but if you don't work as a team you won't win."

Troy was in a sulk. "I'm not coming no more," he said loudly to Zack, pulling on his track suit top. How dare they criticise him?

"They're only telling you how to do it because you're good," said Zack.

"Could have fooled me," said Troy moodily.

He put up with it for couple of months, then something the coach said put his back up and he swore he wouldn't go back again. But he was bored without Zack to go around town with. One Saturday when Zack came round he shoved his kit into a bag.

"Might as well go. But don't anyone tell me what to do, that's all!"

Chapter 3

When he got there Bob Gregg was in the changing room.

"I'm looking for some talent to train up," he said, his keen blue eyes searching the room. "Troy, where have you been? Had my eye on you right from the start. Natural ball sense. Nimble footwork."

"Lots of practice running from the police," said Troy with a grin. They didn't realise it wasn't a joke.

Troy was put into the new team. There were hints that they were being trained up for the Wanderers.

It was not easy being part of a team. He hated it when Gregg yelled at him. But he began to see it wasn't so different from going out with the gang and running rings round the cops. You still have to work together.

He didn't go out making trouble so often now. Bob Gregg's hints were beginning to turn into promises. There could be a future for him as a professional footballer if he wanted to work at it.

"Is he having me on?" he said to Zack. "Just having a cheap laugh?"

"Don't be daft," said Zack. "You're good, and he knows it."

It would mean he couldn't go out clubbing so often. Gregg had warned them all they had to get enough sleep and eat the right stuff. That wasn't so easy.

"Mum, I've got to eat proper," he told her.

"I got you pizza for tonight," said his mum.

"No, proper food," said Troy. "Steaks and that."

"Are you joking?" His mum looked at him suspiciously.

He got his way. The stepdad of the moment might be a wimp, but he had money.

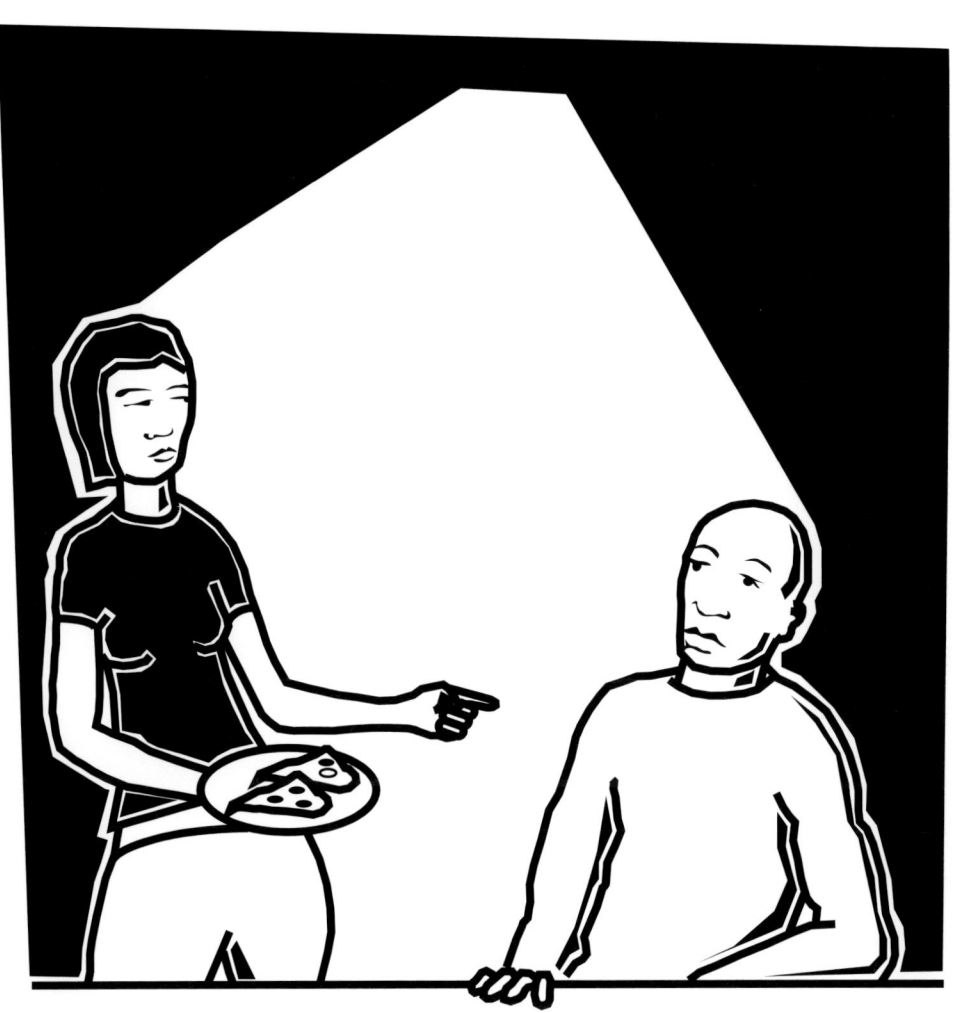

He didn't miss going out and getting pissed at all. Well, not very much.

Zack was round when they heard about the knife amnesty on TV.

"Amnesty!" said Zack. "They'll just take your fingerprints or DNA and then they've got you!"

"Shut up," said Troy. "I'm listening."

For the first time ever he wanted something more than a lifetime spent dodging the police. He never took the knives or the machete out with him now. They were stuck in a bottom drawer in his room. He didn't think he'd ever use them again. But in the back of his mind there had always been the worry that if he chucked them somewhere, the cops would catch up with him for several unsolved stabbings.

Guaranteed no reprisals. Well, that would be fine. If you could trust them.

It was on TV a lot. They even told you how to wrap them up.

"You gonna get rid of yours, Zack?"

Zack stared at him. "You've got to be joking, man. What you gonna do when there's a fight? Stand there like a big girl's blouse? Nah, it's all a police set-up."

Chapter 4

In spite of what Zack said, Troy reckoned it was worth it. He didn't want anything to go wrong with his new football career. Even if the police did keep tabs on him, he'd got Gregg to be a character witness for him now.

Anyway, they went on about it so much on the TV. No further action, they kept saying, and there was no reason to suppose they were lying. Even the papers didn't say anything, and you could bet your footie boots that if there was anything dodgy The *Mirror* would have jumped onto it.

He brought them out of the drawer. Good thing his Mum never did any cleaning round the house. She'd have gone mental if she'd found them.

Nice lot, they were. He'd got the flick knife from Bonzer, one of the gang who hung out with drug dealers. And there was a cool chef's knife that he'd nicked when they'd done a café once, ages ago. That had a blade that would slice a hair in half – lengthways. He'd never used it – not to cut anyone. Only to threaten them. When people saw it they tended to run the other way.

There were a couple of others. Small enough to hide in your clothes when you went out. Quick to flash. Quicker to hide away again.

And the machete. It was a long time since he'd used that. Got it from a West Indian guy he used to hang around with. It was as mean as the devil. Wicked, man.

He felt the weight of it in his hand. Felt the balance. It was a good weapon, that. You could do a lot of damage with that.

But he wasn't out for doing damage to anyone now.

He was going to be a footballer. A good one. Maybe even, one day, a great one. He sat in the room and dreamed of being another Wayne Rooney, the knives strewn round his feet.

The bang of the front door made his heart jump into his mouth. It was only his stepdad coming in. Hurriedly he put them back into the drawer.

Tomorrow he would go to the police.

Chapter 5

Troy had forgotten he had a football practice the next day. By the time he'd got back home and had some tea it was really late.

But police stations stay open all night. He could still take the knives down there. He could wait till tomorrow, but he wanted to get rid of them now. He'd made up his mind and didn't want to change it.

His mobile went. It was Zack.

"Coming up the pub tonight, Troy?"

"Yeah, man. Could do with a jar. Just got something to do first. Where shall I meet you?"

He had to go now, before he met up with Zack.

He wrapped them up safely, like it told you to on the TV. He pulled out the inner bag of cornflakes from their cardboard outside and used the card to go round the blades. Yesterday's *Sun* went round the cardboard. Mum had left a Tesco bag on the worktop. It was just the right size to drop them in.

It was quite heavy, but nobody would know what he was carrying. He could easily have been coming home from the shop with a few microwave dinners.

The police station was on the way to the pub where he was meeting Zack. He just hoped he didn't meet any of his mates on the way. He could just imagine what they'd say if they knew he was taking his weapons to the fuzz!

He went past another pub.

PUBLIC
BAR

It was early in the evening, but already some of the drinkers had had a skin full. He could hear the shouts from the pavement outside. His experienced ear told him they were happy drunks – so far. But the noise was getting nearer the door. It sounded as if they were ready to move on somewhere else.

He didn't want to get caught up in it. Even happy drunks might get in the way of what he had to do. And he couldn't risk anything, not with all that stuff in his bag. Moods could change in a flash, and he wouldn't be able to get his weapons out quickly enough.

He had to stop himself thinking like that. He wasn't going to get caught up in anything, okay?

"Turn in your knife before someone turns it on you," they said. It was plastered all over the papers. So yeah, that's what he was going to do.

There was an alley just across the road. It was a short cut to one of the pubs he and Zack used to go to before they got banned. He'd only have to turn back a short way to get to the police station, then he could go and meet Zack.

But instead of escaping the happy drunks, he was trapped.

Trapped by a desperate, silent fight that was going on at the end of the alley.

Chapter 6

There was a small, glimmering light. It was never bright enough in the alley. But it was enough for Troy to see them. Someone pushed up against the dark wall. Others beating the hell out of him.

And it was enough for Zack to see him.

"Troy!" he croaked. "For godsake, help me!"

There were four against him. Troy knew them. Real heavy guys. But he'd fought them before. Even two against the four of them they'd got a good chance.

He didn't think. Not more than he needed to size up what was happening.

He needed weapons. They were here.

34

Bloody wrappings! He'd done them up too well. He ripped the sellotape off the newspaper. The machete was easy to get out. Bigger. More room for fingers to get under the paper.

"Troy!" Zack's voice was gasping, like he was being strangled.

Troy kicked the bag away. The blade of his machete gleamed in the faint light.

He lifted it above his head and roared into action.

They weren't expecting the blade. Two of them got cut badly before they had time to turn round. They were trying to keep hold of Zack. But once one of them let go, Zack got in there and his powerful fists smashed into a face. There was a satisfying crunch of cheekbone. Troy followed with a kick between someone's legs and a swift slice across his arm.

Then somehow it all went wrong.

He lost his grip on the machete and one of the heavies managed to grab it. He felt a searing pain through the back of his leg. The leg wouldn't hold him any more and he fell to the ground. Zack screamed as the thugs ran out of the alley.

As the police sirens wailed and the dull light of the alley changed to the flicker of blue, Zack gasped, "Thanks, mate. They've gone!"

They had also gone with Troy's Tesco bag.

"Great," Troy thought through the pain. "No incriminating evidence."

Except for the machete. But that had the other guy's fingerprints on it now.

It was victory.

Except that it wasn't.

The police had nothing on them. Zack had got jumped on in the alley – the attack wasn't anything to do with him. The heavies had thought he was someone else.

Zack got a broken arm – the biggest guy had kicked him as they fled. Troy had come off worse. The machete slice had taken a good bit off his calf muscle.

They did say he would be able to walk again.

But his football career was over before it had properly begun.

Glossary

amnesty	a time when people can give weapons or drugs to the police, or admit that they have done something wrong, without being punished
big girl's blouse	slang meaning wimp, weakling
bombing	running very quickly
character witness	a witness who swears to the good standing of another person
dope	slang for cannabis
draw	slang for cannabis
fluke	something good that happens only because of luck or chance
footie	slang for football
fuzz	slang for police
incriminating	something that makes someone seem guilty of a crime
keep tabs on	to watch something or someone carefully
pep talk	a short speech to encourage people to work harder or try to win a game or contest
put his back up	to annoy someone
poncy	slang for unmasculine
reprisals	activity against someone else, often as a punishment
searing	burning
smack	slang for heroin
victory	when you win a game, competition, election or war